Embracing Life's Challenges with Love, Courage, and Positivity.

Raven Harrington

Copyright © Raven Harrington 2024

All Rights Reserved

All rights reserved. No part of this publication may be reproduced, distributed, or transmitted in any form or by any means, including photocopying, recording, or other electronic or mechanical methods, without the author's prior written permission, except in the case of brief quotations embodied in critical reviews and certain other non-commercial uses permitted by copyright law. For permission requests, please get in touch with the author.

Contents

Dedication i

About the Author ii

Introduction 2

Chapter 1 Relieving Stress and Anxiety 4

Chapter 2 Learning to Love Myself 7

Chapter 3 Trust and Forgiveness 10

Chapter 4 Healing Grief: Letting Go for Renewal 15

Chapter 5 Finding Health: A Journey to Healing 19

Chapter 6 Overcoming Insomnia and Health Challenges 24

Chapter 7 Self-Esteem and Courage 27

Chapter 8 Letting Go of Grudges 31

Chapter 9 Power of Positivity 34

Dedication

I am dedicating this book to my son, Christian. This kid is an amazing young man, and I am so proud of his accomplishments. His greatest achievement was his certification as a forklift driver in his junior year. He has many other achievements, but this is the one that inspired me to write my book.

About the Author

Hello. My name is Raven Harrington. I am the author of Embracing Life's Challenges with Love, Courage, and Positivity. I was born in Mississippi, in a small town known for its great hospitality and good food. I now reside in the state of California. My profession is in the medical field where my goal is to care for my clients, helping them with daily routines of life.

I do this by embracing love and kindness to each one. In results of improvement, my life has been a rollercoaster. I am a survivor of being violated, of being in a bad car accident and being diagnosed with Anemia. I overcame these traumas by embracing them with love, courage, and positivity.

I won't allow my traumas to trump my success.

THE BEST WAY TO REACT BEFORE A PROBLEM IS SILENCE OF YOUR TONGUE AND MIND. IT IS EASY SAID THAN DONE BUT WE HAVE TO DO IT IN ORDER TO HAVE PEACE.

Introduction

Raven stood at the crossroads of her own existence, a place defined by a singular moment that divided her life into the "before" and "after." The catalyst for this profound transformation was an unexpected collision with fate – a life-altering car accident that would reshape her perspective on well-being, resilience, and the intricate dance between body and mind.

Before the accident, Raven's life unfolded in a rhythm devoid of conscious health focus. Days blended into each other, each one a blurry echo of the last. The pursuit of physical and mental well-being was a distant notion, preoccupied by the hustle and bustle of a life lived on autopilot. Little did she know that the universe had other plans for her, plans that would be set in motion with the screeching sound of brakes and the shattering impact of metal against metal, a reality that would soon be altered and shattered along with the glass of her car windows.

The aftermath of the accident painted a picture for Raven's metamorphosis. In the wreckage, amidst the debris of twisted metal, she found herself facing with the fragility of life and the unexpected turns it could take. It was here, amidst the chaos, that the seeds of transformation were sown.

Post-accident struggles became a testing ground for Raven's resilience. Physical pain intertwined with emotional turmoil as she navigated the arduous path of recovery. It was in these moments of vulnerability that she discovered two unlikely allies – exercise and meditation.

The tone is set for a journey that transcends the boundaries of personal experience, inviting readers to reflect on their own relationship with well-being. This book is not just a prelude but a promise – a promise of a deeper exploration into Raven's ongoing quest for well-being.

The following chapters intricately and delicately peel back the layers of Raven's experience, revealing the profound impact of these holistic practices on her journey to well-being.

Chapter 1
Relieving Stress and Anxiety

I want to share a story with you, a moment that changed everything for me. It was March 3rd 2021. I remember the date like it was yesterday. It was morning and the sun shone brightly. I was driving on the freeway, and got stuck in a traffic jam. People were honking their horns and being overall impatient. Meanwhile, I was listening to a song on the local radio in my car. I was driving slowly in the middle lane, singing along to an old song that reminded me of my youth, when all of a sudden, I felt a jerk.

The sudden jerk propelled me forward, and I hit my head on the steering wheel, even though I was wearing a seatbelt. My car weaved towards the right and hit the metal guardrail.

The impact was so sudden it shook me to my very core. At first, I didn't realize what had happened. I was hit from behind and the truck push me all the way over to the car pool lane. I tried to turn my neck to comprehend what had happened. As soon as I tried turning my neck, I felt a searing pain in my neck and back. The accident left me with bulging discs on my neck and back. After the paramedics arrived and took me out using the 'jaws of life', they informed me that a car had rammed me from behind, totaling my car.

It was a life-altering car accident, one of those unexpected events that can reshape your whole life. Recovering from the accident was difficult, to say the least. It is not at all like they show it in the movies.

Recovery takes more than just determination. It takes willpower and courage. I had to change my overall sedentary lifestyle to an active one. At first, it was just for the sake of recovery. But then I started reading about how exercise and meditation helps the mind stay sharp and the body heal quicker from any and all injuries. Over time, I adopted this new lifestyle and have never looked back since.

But along with healing came something unexpected – a feeling born from the collision of metal and fate – a feeling of being trapped, like the space around me was closing in. The accident left me with this new kind of fear. As the shadows of the accident cast their devastating hold on my psyche, I realized the accident had damaged more than just my physical well-being. It also damaged my mental wellbeing.

I started to realize that I was feeling uncomfortable in my own car in the middle of a traffic jam, even though nothing was happening. I was unable to sit peacefully in a car especially when it started to rain heavily or when a wind would blow strongly. I started to have panic attacks. This is where meditation came to my rescue. Later, I discovered I had developed claustrophobia. However, meditation showed me that taking deep breaths could be really calming and helpful. This neat little trick can do wonders to calm you down.

Before that, my days were just routine stuff, no big focus on staying healthy or anything like that. But then, the crash happened. Glass shattered, metal twisted, and suddenly, life wasn't the same. It made me think about how fragile things are and how a single moment can turn everything upside down. Recovery after the accident wasn't easy. It felt like I was climbing a steep hill, full of pain and uncertainty.

Then, I found two things that helped me a lot: exercise and meditation. Exercise became my escape, a way to release all the built-up tension. Sweating it out somehow made me feel stronger, both physically and mentally. And meditation? That was like a peaceful break for my mind. It helped me deal with all the worries that wouldn't leave me alone.

As I faced personal challenges, exercise and meditation became my guides, showing me a way to take care of both my mind and body. Meditation became a balm for my wounded soul, a practice that allowed me to confront the echoes of the recent trauma. Through meditation, I found solace and relief from the trauma that threatened to engulf me.

This chapter is just the start, a sneak peek into my journey. It's a promise that we're going to dive deeper into how I learned to deal with life's ups and downs. So, as you read, imagine you're right there with me on this adventure of facing challenges with love, courage, and positivity.

Chapter 2
Learning to Love Myself

As I walk down the memory lane of my past relationships, I can't help but notice the twists and turns, the moments of joy, and the painful echoes of heartbreak. It's a journey filled with lessons, and in those lessons, I discovered the profound importance of *self-love* and *self-care*.

In love, I always gave my all. I poured my heart into every connection, hoping for a reciprocal of affection. But, as life would have it, the storms came. Relationships soured, and I found myself unfairly carrying the blame. It was like holding an umbrella in a hurricane — futile, exhausting, and, at times, seemingly never-ending.

Reflecting on those moments, I realized that I had neglected something crucial — *myself*. It wasn't about being selfish but about understanding that self-love is the foundation on which any healthy relationship stands. So, I decided to embark on a journey, not through distant lands but through the corridors of my own heart.

In the quiet spaces of my soul, I discovered my spiritual compass. For me, it was a belief in God. In the embrace of my spirituality, I found a form of self-care that went beyond bubble baths and spa days. It was a refuge where I could be vulnerable, find peace, and draw the strength needed to face life's challenges.

Society, with its watchful eyes and demanding expectations, has a way of nudging us to seek approval, to be liked and loved by everyone. It's a magnetic pull that can lead us astray if we're not careful. I confess I fell into that trap, too. The desire to fit in, to be accepted, sometimes overshadowed the importance of my own mental well-being.

But life has a way of nudging us back on track, and in my case, it was a wake-up call. I realized that prioritizing the opinions of others over my own mental health was a precarious balance. It was like walking on a tightrope, and I was risking falling into an abyss of self-doubt.

So, I took a step back. I began to understand that societal approval is fleeting, like a passing breeze. What endures is our mental and emotional well-being. In the quiet moments of self-examination, I found a powerful realization unfolding — the essence of *self-love*. It wasn't about arrogance or narcissism; it was a humble acknowledgment of my own worthiness. In embracing my imperfections, I discovered a reservoir of strength that I never knew existed.

This journey towards self-love is not a sprint; it's a marathon. It requires patience, understanding, and a willingness to face the shadows within. It's about being your own best friend, forgiving your mistakes, and understanding that you're a work in progress. In a world that sometimes feels like it's spinning too fast, self-love becomes the anchor, grounding us in our authenticity.

So, dear reader, as you navigate the complexities of relationships and societal expectations, remember this — the ultimate form of well-being is not found in the approval of others but in your own self-appreciation. It's a journey, a beautiful one, filled with bumps and detours, but it leads to a place where you can embrace life's challenges with love, courage, and an unwavering sense of positivity.

Chapter 3
Trust and Forgiveness

It's difficult to talk about trust and forgiveness without delving into the darkest corners of my own past, where betrayal and pain intertwined, threatening to consume me. It was a cold winter evening during my second year of college when my world was turned upside down. The incident that unfolded would leave scars on my heart, testing my belief in humanity and challenging the very essence of trust.

In those early days, trust came easy to me. I believed that people were inherently good, that friendships were unbreakable, and that promises were meant to be kept. Little did I know that life had its own set of lessons to teach me.

It happened on a Thursday, a day that started like any other. Classes, laughter, and the anticipation of the weekend ahead. I had a close friend, someone I trusted implicitly. We shared secrets, dreams, and the mundane details of our everyday lives. But that evening, the fabric of that trust would be ripped apart.

In the aftermath of a night that left me broken and violated, I faced an agonizing decision. I chose not to turn in the person who had committed this heinous act against me. Fear, shame, and the harsh judgments society often imposes on survivors kept me silent. The weight of that secret, like an anchor, dragged me down into a sea of despair.

Eventually, I was faced with a daunting task. My parents had started to notice the change in my behavior, and soon, circumstances forced me to reveal to my parents about the unimaginable pain I had endured. The words hung heavy in the air, shattering their world as much as it had shattered mine. The support they offered was unwavering, but the scars ran deep, prompting me to make a painful decision—to leave my hometown in pursuit of healing and a fresh start.

Bitterness crept into my heart like a relentless shadow. Trust shattered, and I found myself questioning everyone and everything. The world that once seemed warm and inviting turned cold and hostile. I withdrew, building walls around me, determined not to let anyone close enough to hurt me again.

Days turned into weeks and weeks into months, but the bitterness lingered. It became a constant companion, shaping my interactions, clouding my judgment, and casting a dark shadow over my once vibrant spirit. I was imprisoned by my own resentment, unable to move forward.

It was in the depths of this darkness that I stumbled upon an unexpected source of strength — Faith in God. I let God into my life, not as a desperate plea for answers, but as a source of strength to face the shadows that clung to me. In prayer, I discovered a refuge where judgment didn't exist and where I could pour out the pain that I thought would forever define me. In those moments, I discovered a resilience within myself that I never knew existed.

Jesus became a beacon of forgiveness in my life. As I delved into the teachings of compassion and mercy, I realized that forgiveness wasn't just a concept; it was a transformative force. The forgiveness Jesus extended to those who tormented him became a guiding light. If he could forgive, then perhaps, in time, I could too.

Releasing the pain that clung to me like a relentless shadow wasn't a one-time event. It was a gradual process, like peeling away layers of darkness to let the light in. With each prayer, I took a step closer to understanding that holding onto anger was like carrying a heavy burden that weighed down my soul.

The turning point came when I made a conscious decision to forgive the person who had betrayed me. It wasn't easy, and the wounds were still fresh, but I knew that forgiveness was the only path to liberation. Forgiveness became the key that unlocked the door to my own prison, and as I forgave, I felt the weight lifting from my shoulders.

A sense of catharsis started to wash over me. It was a release, a letting go of the bitterness that had consumed my being. In that process, I discovered the true power of forgiveness — the ability to reclaim my sense of self.

Forgiving the person who had caused me so much pain wasn't an endorsement of their actions. It was a conscious choice to free myself from the chains of hatred and resentment. It was about reclaiming my identity from the clutches of victimhood and choosing to define myself by my strength, not my suffering. It meant acknowledging that we are all imperfect beings capable of both great kindness and deep hurt. In forgiving, I embraced the imperfections of humanity and, in turn, my own.

Jesus forgave those who crucified him, and in that spirit, I found the courage to forgive my tormentor. It wasn't an easy journey, and there were moments when the wounds still felt fresh.

The liberating power of releasing what cannot be held is a lesson that has stayed with me since that transformative period of my life. Trust, once broken, can be rebuilt. Forgiveness, once granted, can be a source of strength rather than weakness.

In sharing my journey from anguish to forgiveness, I hope to inspire others to find the courage to release the burdens they carry. Trusting again may seem daunting, and forgiving may appear impossible, but within these challenges lies the opportunity for growth, healing, and the rediscovery of the beauty of life.

As I stand on the other side of that dark chapter, I carry with me the scars of betrayal, but they no longer define me. Instead, they serve as a testament to the resilience of the human spirit and the transformative power of trust and forgiveness. Embracing life's challenges with love, courage, and positivity means acknowledging the pain but also choosing to rise above it, allowing the light of forgiveness to guide us forward.

I have found a strength within that refuses to be extinguished.

Chapter 4
Healing Grief: Letting Go for Renewal

Life, with its twists and turns, has a way of teaching us profound lessons through the tapestry of joy and sorrow. For me, the canvas of my life was painted with vibrant hues, but it also bore the shadows of profound losses that tested the limits of my spirit. In 2006, the year etched in my memory, I faced a cascade of sorrow as the hands of time took away the pillar of my world—my father.

My father, a sturdy oak in the garden of my life, stood tall and resolute. His laughter echoed in the corridors of our home, a comforting melody that defined my childhood. He was the guiding force, the one who imparted life's lessons with a gentle touch and a heart full of love. His sudden departure left a void that seemed insurmountable.

The last time I faced a sorrow of this kind was back in the mid-90s. If memory serves me right it was 1995. My grandfather, a wise soul whose eyes sparkled with the wisdom of years, joined the cosmic dance of stars. We shared a sacred space in the garden, a patch of earth where time seemed to stand still. It was here, amid the fragrant blossoms and the rustling leaves, that we found joy in our shared moments. His stories were my bedtime tales, and his presence was a sanctuary of love.

The garden, once a haven of laughter and shared dreams, became a poignant reminder of the ones who had graced it with their presence. Each petal held a memory, each breeze whispered a tale, and the shadows of their absence lingered in every corner. The weight of grief settled over me like a heavy fog, obscuring the brightness of life.

Years rolled by, and life went on. But life relentless in its journey, presented new losses. On November 14^{th,} 2022, the day of my birthday, a day when everyone celebrates life with their loved ones, my life was once again filled with grief. My dearest aunt passed away. Three months later, after grieving her, just as we thought we were on the road to an emotional recovery, life decided to place another emotional hurdle our way. On February 5^{th,} 2023, my dear uncle passed away.

The passing of my aunt and uncle, dear souls who had woven threads of care and warmth into the fabric of our family. The waves of grief, now familiar, crashed over me once again, threatening to pull me under. My uncle was a great man. He loved his children and would make everyone that he loved laugh and would laugh heartily with them as well. He was a local mechanic and one of the best. There wasn't a mechanical riddle that he could not solve. And my aunt was a sweet, sweet woman who loved her family and children dearly.

We cried together, hugged silently, and found comfort in shared memories. The laughter from the past, the meals we had together, and the support during tough times - all of it became like patches stitching us together in our sadness. We faced the storms as a family, supporting each other when things got tough.

The garden, once a place of memories, turned into a living proof of our strength. We took care of it, nurturing the flowers that represented the love we still felt for those we lost. Their laughter turned into music, guiding us as we moved through life.

Healing takes time. It's like taking care of wounds, accepting that feelings come and go, and deciding to let go of the pain. It's a journey through the ups and downs, where every step forward feels like a win over the sadness.

My family's love was like medicine for the pain. It went beyond life and death, showing me that true love never really ends. Remembering the good times became a way of starting fresh. We didn't cry in sadness but smiled, knowing we had something beautiful in our memories.

As years passed, my life's garden changed. The losses, once heavy weights pulling me down, turned into wings lifting me higher. Grief, though still there, became a gentle reminder of the love that shaped me. I carry their spirits with me, guiding me through life's challenges.

Through this process, I've uncovered a valuable life lesson — the art of letting go. Letting go of things that no longer serve a purpose, shedding the weight of unnecessary burdens, and freeing myself from the grip of the past. It's a lesson in lightness, where I release what I don't need to make room for the beauty of the present and the promise of tomorrow.

The wounds of the past, once open and raw, have healed. The scars remain, a testament to the battles fought, and the strength gained. I've emerged on the other side, not untouched by the pain but stronger because of it. The journey through grief has taught me resilience, the capacity to withstand the storms, and find sunlight on the other side.

Love, I've come to understand, is not just a fleeting emotion but a guiding force. It leads my heart and shapes my actions. I've learned to let love be my compass, navigating the complexities of life with compassion and understanding. Through the challenges, love has been my constant, a beacon that illuminates the path ahead.

In embracing life's challenges with love, courage, and positivity, I've learned that grief is just a part of being human. It's not about forgetting but finding the strength to carry memories with grace. My life's garden, now blooming with resilience, stands as proof that love can endure even when faced with loss.

I've not only healed from the wounds of the past but have also discovered the limitless potential of a heart fueled by love.

Chapter 5
Finding Health: A Journey to Healing

It was a tranquil Friday afternoon by the duck pond when the ordinary transformed into the extraordinary. The serenity of the scene was interrupted by an unexpected wave of dizziness, and the world around me blurred. Legs that had been steady moments ago betrayed me, and I found myself collapsing near the pond's edge.

The concerned quacks of nearby ducks seemed to blend with the worried voices of compassionate strangers. In that moment of vulnerability, concerned and considerate strangers rushed to my aid; kind-hearted individuals who were enjoying the same slice of nature as I was just a few waking moments ago. They swiftly gathered, offering a helping hand, and with quick thinking, called for assistance. It was a reminder that in life's unpredictable narrative, the supporting cast can emerge from the most unexpected places.

Hospital walls replaced the idyllic pond as I came to grips with the severity of my situation. My sister and brother-in-law stood as pillars of strength, their unwavering presence a comfort amid the clinical surroundings. In the sterile confines of the hospital, as I lay on the crisp white sheets, the gravity of my situation sank in.

The doctors, with their reassuring yet concerned expressions, explained that my collapse was a result of dangerously low blood levels. It was a revelation that brought the fragility of my health into sharp focus. In the days that followed, I underwent a blood transfusion and received four bags of calcium, a lifeline that replenished what my body desperately needed. It was a stark reminder that even the seemingly routine can take an unexpected turn, underscoring the urgency of our commitment to health.

Meanwhile, daily phone calls from my son and mother became lifelines, connecting me to the outside world and infusing hope into each conversation.

As I navigated the road to recovery, I found strength in the unwavering support of my loved ones. My son, a beacon of resilience, stood by my side, offering a steadying presence in the face of uncertainty. His father, too, extended a helping hand, reminding me that even in life's most challenging moments, we are not alone. It was a testament to the power of familial bonds and the love that threads through the tapestry of our lives.

In the quiet moments of reflection, gratitude filled my heart. I thanked God who guides our destinies for the compassionate strangers who called for help on that fateful Tuesday, for the skilled healthcare professionals who tended to my well-being, and for the love that surrounded me in the form of my family. November 15, 2023, became a date etched not in fear but in resilience, a marker of a pivotal moment that deepened my appreciation for the precious gift of life

In the days that followed my collapse, I found myself contemplating the nature of these silent foes. Why do they persist, and what role does our lifestyle play in their persistence? It became clear that a proactive approach to health is not just a choice but a responsibility we owe to ourselves and those who care about us.

Chronic illnesses, like uninvited guests, often linger on the fringes of our awareness, waiting for the opportune moment to make their presence known. They are stealthy adversaries, and it's easy to underestimate their impact until they forcefully announce their presence.

This incident marked the beginning of my journey into understanding the profound importance of our physical health. It was a wake-up call that prompted me to reevaluate my lifestyle and prioritize the well-being of this vessel that carries us through the journey of life.

In the wake of that transformative hospital stay, the journey toward holistic well-being expanded to embrace the crucial role of nourishment. I embarked on a mission to cultivate a healthier relationship with food, realizing that a balanced diet was not just a choice but a cornerstone of vitality. It wasn't about restrictive diets or deprivation; rather, it was a mindful approach to choosing foods that nourished not only the body but also the spirit.

I discovered that a healthy diet is not a rigid prescription but a harmonious symphony of colorful vegetables, lean proteins, and whole grains. It's about savoring the richness of natural flavors and embracing moderation as a guiding principle.

In this ongoing journey, I learned that a healthy diet complements the rhythm of regular exercise and the serenity of meditation. It is a trinity, a collective force that propels us toward a life filled with energy, resilience, and joy. So, as I continue to tread the path of well-being, I do so with a plate full of gratitude, savoring the wisdom that what we eat is not just sustenance but a celebration of life itself.

Maintaining good health doesn't require complex rituals or drastic lifestyle changes. It begins with the simplicity of regular exercise. A brisk walk, a few stretches, or even a short dance in the living room – these are not Herculean tasks but small steps that can make a significant difference. Our bodies crave movement, and in the dance between stillness and motion, we find the rhythm of well-being.

Meditation, too, emerged as a powerful ally on my journey to healing. In the midst of life's chaos, taking a few moments to quiet the mind proved to be a balm for the soul. It doesn't demand a mountain retreat or hours of solitude; a quiet corner and a few minutes of focused breathing are often enough to cultivate a sense of inner calm.

Equally important is our relationship with healthcare professionals. Open lines of communication with those who dedicate their lives to our well-being can be transformative. Regular check-ups, honest conversations about our concerns, and a willingness to embrace preventive measures form the foundation of a robust health strategy.

As I embraced these simple yet powerful practices, I realized that good health is not a destination but a journey. It's a daily commitment to making choices that honor our bodies and minds. It's about understanding that our well-being is not just a personal matter but a shared responsibility, a ripple effect that extends beyond ourselves.

So, here's to embracing life's challenges with love, courage, and positivity – starting with the vessel that carries us through it all. May we walk this journey of health together, one step at a time, with compassion for ourselves and those who lend a helping hand when we stumble. After all, in the dance of life, our health is the melody that keeps us moving forward.

Chapter 6
Overcoming Insomnia and Health Challenges

As I sit down to share this chapter with you, I find myself reflecting on a time when sleep was an elusive visitor. Nights seemed to stretch endlessly, and my mind was a battlefield of worries and regrets. Insomnia, it turns out, is not just a lack of sleep; it's a silent struggle with the ghosts of our past.

It was a period of my life when I found myself trapped in the web of overthinking. Every mistake, every wrong turn, played on repeat in the theater of my mind. Sleep became a distant dream, and rest was a luxury that I could hardly afford. I knew I had to confront the shadows that haunted me, but letting go is often easier said than done.

In my journey to overcome insomnia, I discovered a profound truth: simplicity is the key to untangling the complex knots of our thoughts. It was about finding a way to declutter the mind and make room for peace. This chapter is a testament to the power of simplicity in overcoming the challenges life throws at us, especially when it comes to our health.

The first step on my path to better sleep was acknowledging that I needed to let go. It's incredible how much emotional baggage we carry from our past, and it often manifests itself in our inability to find rest. I began by facing my fears and regrets head-on, looking at them in the light of a new day. It was not easy, but it was necessary.

As I navigated this internal landscape, I realized that simplicity could be a soothing balm for the soul. I started incorporating small yet meaningful changes in my daily routine. Regular exercise became a non-negotiable part of my day. A simple walk in the fresh air or a few minutes of stretching did wonders for my overall well-being.

Hydration, too, played a pivotal role. Increasing my water intake not only benefited my physical health but also had a surprisingly positive impact on my mental state. It was as if each sip of water washed away a bit of the heaviness that had settled within me.

A good amount of rest for the body is not just essential; it's a soothing elixir for the mind. I discovered the profound impact of a full night's sleep, approximately nine hours, on my overall well-being. This rejuvenating rest enriched my life, boosting my productivity and providing me with the resilience needed to face life's challenges head-on.

Yet, the most transformative aspect of my journey was the simplest of all – prayer. I turned to God, not in elaborate rituals or complicated chants, but in the quiet sincerity of my heart. It was a conversation, a release of my burdens to a higher power. In those moments of vulnerability, I found strength. It wasn't about demanding a cure for my insomnia; it was about seeking guidance and finding strength in the divine.

The more I delved into this practice, the more I realized that forgiveness was a crucial component of my healing. As I pondered during my moments of meditation, I began to see that forgiving those who had hurt me, whether intentionally or unintentionally, was the path to peace. It was not about excusing their actions but releasing the hold they had on my mind.

Forgiveness, I discovered, was a gift to myself. It allowed me to break free from the chains of resentment and anger. It opened the door to a profound sense of peace, a peace that became the foundation for restful nights and a rejuvenated spirit.

In sharing this part of my life with you, I want to emphasize that the struggle with insomnia and health challenges is universal. I ask and invite you, dear reader, to ponder what might be causing your own struggles with insomnia. As I identified my own causes – trauma from the past, injuries from my accident, stress, and overthinking – I realized that each of us carries unique burdens. It's an invitation to confront these issues head-on, to acknowledge them in the light of day, and to work towards healing.

In sharing this part of my life with you, I want to emphasize that the struggle with insomnia and health challenges is universal. We all carry burdens, regrets, and worries that weigh us down. But in embracing simplicity – in acknowledging the power of a walk, a sip of water, and a heartfelt prayer – we can find the strength to overcome.

Life's challenges are inevitable, but our response to them is within our control. It's about choosing simplicity over complexity, about finding courage in small, consistent steps. As you read this chapter, I invite you to reflect on the simplicity that can bring peace to your own life, allowing you to embrace each day with love, courage, and positivity.

Chapter 7
Self-Esteem and Courage

Let me take you back to a time when my days were a maze of comparisons, each turn leading to a dead-end of self-doubt. It was an era where the grass always seemed greener on the other side, and my self-worth crumbled beneath the weight of incessant comparisons. The more I looked at others, the less I saw in myself.

It's funny how these comparisons sneak into our lives, often masquerading as harmless reflections. I found myself measuring my worth against the achievements, appearances, and seemingly perfect lives of those around me. It became a game I didn't realize I was playing, and slowly, it eroded the very core of who I was.

The toll on my well-being was palpable. Anxiety became a relentless companion, whispering doubts and insecurities into the quiet corners of my mind. Relationships, too, bore the brunt of this incessant comparison. How can one fully connect with others when the lens through which we view ourselves is distorted by the shadows of comparison?

One day, as I stood at the crossroads of self-reflection, a simple yet profound truth dawned upon me – the importance of living authentically. I realized that the shackles of comparison were hindering not just my progress but my very essence. It was time to break free, to embrace my unique path with all its quirks and imperfections.

The journey to authenticity was not without its challenges. It required a courageous leap into the unknown, away from the comfortable familiarity of comparisons.

In the tangled web of comparisons, relationships bore the weight of my scrutinizing gaze. Whether it was the romance flickering in others' lives or the familial bonds painted with shades of perfection, I found myself constantly measuring my relationships against these idealized images. The more I compared, the more it seemed like I was destined to fall short, and this overthinking cast a shadow on the genuine connections I had. It took a brave heart to untangle these threads of comparison from the delicate fabric of my relationships.

Courage became my ally, the sturdy companion that helped me dismantle the walls built by societal expectations and peer pressure. It was the courage to stand tall in my own truth, unapologetically and authentically.

In the journey towards authenticity, I discovered a liberating truth – there will always be haters. The world, with its kaleidoscope of opinions, is not short on critics. Instead of letting their whispers dampen my spirit, I turned it into fuel. As I embarked on this path of self-discovery and courage, the haters unwittingly became narrators of my success story, their whispers of doubt transforming into echoes of acknowledgment.

In sharing this, I extend a piece of advice to you, dear reader – embrace your uniqueness. The world doesn't need more replicas; it craves the authenticity that only you can bring. Let go of the suffocating weight of comparisons and breathe in the liberating air of self-acceptance. It's a journey, not a destination, but oh, the freedom it brings.

Courage, too, became a beacon in this transformative odyssey. The courage to take risks, to venture into the unknown, and to believe in the possibility of a life lived on your terms. It's not about the absence of fear; rather, it's the audacity to take that next step despite the trembling knees and racing heart.

Success, I learned, was not measured by the yardstick of others but by the milestones achieved on my authentic journey. It was the realization that the path less traveled may be daunting, but it's where the most beautiful stories are written. Each stumble, each fall, became a testament to the courage that propelled me forward.

One big lesson struck me hard – it's not about how long I live; it's about how deep I live each day. Life's unpredictable, and I realized that the true value lies in making each moment count. It's not about the number of days but about the realness we bring to each one. So, here's to facing each day with bravery, weaving the unique story of our lives, and proving, not to the doubters, but to ourselves that our journey, no matter its length, is a celebration of living true and wholeheartedly.

So, as you navigate the twists and turns of your own journey, remember this – the courage to be yourself is the greatest gift you can give to the world. Break free from the chains of comparison, take that leap of faith, and let the echoes of your authentic footsteps reverberate through the tapestry of your life. The world is waiting, not for a perfect copy, but for the uniquely beautiful masterpiece that is you.

Chapter 8
Letting Go of Grudges

Have you ever thought about the weight we carry when we hold onto grudges? It's like carrying a bag full of rocks – heavy, burdensome, and, after a while, it starts to wear you down. I often found myself wondering, what if we could lighten that load? What if we could release the grip of anger and resentment?

It was a question that echoed in my mind one day, causing me to pause and reflect on the power of forgiveness. The thought struck me like a gentle breeze, inviting me to consider a profound choice: Would I regret more the death of someone I held a grudge against or the missed chance to reconcile while they were alive? It was a stark realization that life, with its unpredictable turns, offers no guarantees, and the opportunity to mend bridges may slip away like sand through our fingers.

As I grappled with this notion, I turned to a source of solace – my faith. Seeking guidance from God, I embarked on a journey to find the strength to forgive. It wasn't an easy path; forgiveness never is. It requires peeling away layers of hurt, acknowledging pain, and finding a way to release the grip that anger holds on our hearts.

In my pursuit of understanding forgiveness, I delved into the teachings of Jesus. His words echoed with a profound simplicity: "Forgive, and you will be forgiven." It struck me that forgiveness is not just an act of kindness toward others; it is a gift we give to ourselves. It's a key that unlocks the chains of resentment, allowing us to step into a realm of healing and freedom.

His teachings weren't just words on ancient pages; they were living echoes of a forgiveness so vast that it embraced even those who inflicted unimaginable pain upon him. The crucifixion, a symbol of cruelty and suffering, became a canvas for an act of forgiveness that transcended time. As the nails pierced his flesh, Jesus, in his divine compassion, forgave those who tortured and crucified him. It was an act so monumental that it echoes through centuries, a testament to the boundless capacity of forgiveness.

My personal journey toward forgiveness involved acknowledging the harm inflicted, but instead of letting it fester like an open wound, I chose to let go. It wasn't about condoning the actions or pretending they didn't hurt; rather, it was a conscious decision to release the grip of resentment and grant myself the peace that forgiveness brings.

As I navigated this transformative act, I discovered that forgiveness is not a one-time event but a continual process. It's a daily choice to resist the pull of bitterness and embrace the freedom that comes with releasing grudges. The burden lifted, and the air around me felt lighter, as if a storm had passed, leaving behind a calm that I hadn't known in years.

This chapter isn't about preaching the moral high ground of forgiveness; it's about sharing a journey, a simple yet profound exploration of the human heart. It's an invitation for you, dear reader, to consider the weight of grudges you may be carrying. What if, by letting go, you open the door to a brighter, more liberated existence?

In the grand tapestry of life, reconciliation is a thread that weaves connections, healing the fabric of our relationships. It's an acknowledgment that we are all imperfect beings, capable of causing pain and, at the same time, capable of profound transformation through forgiveness.

So, as you journey through life, consider the bag of rocks you might be carrying. Are there grudges that could be released, allowing you to walk a little lighter? Forgiveness is not about forgetting; it's about choosing freedom over the weight of resentment, about embracing life's challenges with love, courage, and positivity.

Chapter 9
Power of Positivity

As I reflect on the journey we've taken together, a resounding truth emerges – the incredible power that positivity holds in shaping our lives. It's not just about wearing a smile or painting everything with a rosy hue; it's a transformative force that influences our well-being, relationships, and the very essence of our existence.

Maintaining a positive outlook is not about ignoring life's challenges; it's about facing them with a mindset that believes in the possibility of a brighter outcome. I've come to realize that positivity is not a destination but a way of traveling through life, a lens through which we see opportunities instead of obstacles.

A cornerstone of this positive mindset is taking care of our physical well-being. Regular exercise, whether it's a stroll in the park or a dance in the living room, infuses our bodies with vitality. It's not about chasing perfection but about honoring the incredible vessel that carries us through life. Movement is a celebration of life, and in that celebration, we find the energy to tackle challenges with resilience and courage.

Meditation, too, emerged as a steadfast companion on this journey. Amidst the noise of daily life, taking a few moments to quiet the mind is a simple yet powerful act. It's a pause button for the soul, allowing us to find calm in the midst of chaos. Whether it's the gentle rhythm of our breath or the rustling leaves outside our window, meditation connects us to the present moment, grounding us in a space of peace.

Proper hydration, often overlooked in the pursuit of well-being, is another building block of positivity. Water, the elixir of life, is not just a physical necessity but a source of refreshment for our minds and spirits. As I embraced this simple act of self-care, I felt the rejuvenating effects ripple through my days, enhancing my clarity of thought and infusing each moment with a sense of vitality.

Lastly, amidst the fabric of positivity, belief in faith and God stands as a sturdy pillar that provides profound purpose to our existence. In my journey, I found that faith isn't just a set of beliefs but a guiding force that anchors us in times of turbulence. It's a source of solace, a reminder that there's a greater plan unfolding even when the road ahead seems uncertain. Embracing faith infuses life with meaning, allowing us to navigate challenges with a sense of purpose and assurance that there's a higher power steering the ship. Just as the sun rises each morning, faith reminds us that there's a rhythm to life, a purpose that transcends our understanding. It's in the moments of quiet reflection and gratitude that we connect with the divine presence, finding strength and purpose in the belief that we are part of something greater than ourselves. Faith, like a beacon, lights our way through the darkest nights and fuels the flame of positivity that burns brightly within us.

But positivity isn't just about individual practices; it thrives in the environment we create around us. Surrounding ourselves with positivity means nurturing relationships that uplift rather than drain. It's a conscious choice to be with people who celebrate our successes, support us in challenges, and inspire us to be our best selves. The company we keep plays a significant role in shaping our outlook, and by fostering positive connections, we create a fertile ground for optimism to flourish.

A pivotal shift occurred when I redirected my focus from comparing myself to others to embracing my unique journey. The poisonous habit of comparison withered away, making room for the growth of positivity. I began to understand that my journey was uniquely mine, with its own twists and turns, victories, and lessons. Embracing this perspective not only freed me from the shackles of self-doubt but also allowed me to celebrate the accomplishments of others without feeling diminished.

In the symphony of positivity, I've come to understand a profound truth – no one else can pick up your broken pieces and mend them for you. It's a task that falls upon us, a journey of self-discovery and self-healing. Just as a potter shapes clay into a beautiful vessel, we have the power to reshape the broken parts of ourselves. It's not about erasing the cracks but acknowledging them as testaments to resilience and growth. We are the architects of our own restoration, and through each intentional act of self-care, forgiveness, and positivity, we become the artisans of our well-being.

Surrounding ourselves with positive people and energy is akin to basking in the warmth of the sun after a long, cold night. Positive relationships act as gentle hands that lift us when we stumble and celebrate with us when we triumph. By cultivating an environment rich in positivity, we create a fertile ground for personal growth and happiness. It's not about denying life's challenges but facing them with a support system that encourages, inspires, and believes in our ability to rise above. The most crucial step in this journey is recognizing the significance of the company we keep and actively choosing to surround ourselves with those who contribute to our positivity tapestry. After all, in this shared journey called life, the energy we absorb and radiate shapes the very fabric of our existence.

In the grand tapestry of life, each of us holds a unique thread. It's not about who has the longest or most colorful thread; it's about the beauty that emerges when these threads weave together. Our individual journeys, with all their imperfections and triumphs, contribute to the rich mosaic of humanity.

So, as we conclude this exploration of life's challenges with love, courage, and positivity, let's remember that cultivating positivity is not an elusive dream but a tangible reality within our grasp. It's in the small, everyday choices – the smile we share, the steps we take, the words we speak, and the company we keep. In each of these, we find the power to infuse our lives with positivity, transforming challenges into opportunities and embracing the beautiful journey that unfolds before us.

www.ingramcontent.com/pod-product-compliance
Lightning Source LLC
Chambersburg PA
CBHW041153110526
44590CB00027B/4219